**This book belongs to:**

...............................

# We are pleased to recommend
## our counterpart's wonderful coloring books

Thank you for choosing this coloring book!
Please consider leaving a positive review on
Amazon. It would mean a lot to me and help
other customers find the book.
Your feedback is greatly appreciated!

★★★★★

♥ Get Free Printable Coloring Pages ♥
& Join Our Community!

https://linktr.ee/5ideas.publishing

- MAXIMUS PRIME -

THANK YOU!

# ARTWORK 1

0 = Dark Brown

1 = Light Blue

2 = Black

3 = Light Brown

4 = Light Orange

5 = Tan

6 = Dark Orange

7 = Dark Purple

8 = Dark Red

9 = Dark Blue

10 = Yellow

11 = Dark Green

12 = Yellow Green

13 = Bright Green

14 = Sky Blue

15 = Medium Blue

**TIP: USE THE SUGGESTED COLOR PALETTE ON THE BACK COVER FOR YOUR REFERENCE.**

# ARTWORK 2

0 = Light Orange
1 = Dark Orange
2 = Dark Red
3 = Black
4 = Dark Pink
5 = Sky Blue
6 = Tan
7 = Cream
8 = Light Brown
9 = Dark Blue
10 = Pink

**TIP: USE THE SUGGESTED COLOR PALETTE ON THE BACK COVER FOR YOUR REFERENCE.**

# ARTWORK 3

0 = Pink
1 = Cream
2 = Black
3 = Dark Pink
4 = Medium Blue
5 = Dark Red
6 = Dark Purple
7 = Red
8 = Violet
9 = Dark Blue
10 = Sky Blue
11 = Light Blue

**TIP: USE THE SUGGESTED COLOR PALETTE ON THE BACK COVER
FOR YOUR REFERENCE.**

# ARTWORK 4

0 = Black

1 = Yellow

2 = Medium Blue

3 = Tan

4 = Dark Red

5 = Dark Brown

6 = Dark Blue

7 = Light Brown

8 = Dark Grey

9 = Cream

10 = Light Grey

11 = Violet

12 = Sky Blue

# ARTWORK 5

0 = Cream
1 = Dark Brown
2 = Black
3 = Bright Green
4 = Light Brown
5 = Dark Orange
6 = Tan
7 = Dark Red
8 = Light Blue
9 = Medium Green
10 = Dark Green
11 = Violet
12 = Yellow Green

**TIP: USE THE SUGGESTED COLOR PALETTE ON THE BACK COVER
FOR YOUR REFERENCE.**

# ARTWORK 6

0 = Black
1 = Sky Blue
2 = Light Blue
3 = Tan
4 = Dark Green
5 = Dark Orange
6 = Dark Blue
7 = Dark Red
8 = Bright Green
9 = Red
10 = Yellow Green
11 = Dark Brown
12 = Medium Green
13 = Medium Blue
14 = Dark Purple

**TIP: USE THE SUGGESTED COLOR PALETTE ON THE BACK COVER
FOR YOUR REFERENCE.**

# ARTWORK 7

0 = Black
1 = Light Blue
2 = Bright Green
3 = Dark Blue
4 = Light Orange
5 = Yellow Green
6 = Dark Orange
7 = Yellow
8 = Tan
9 = Red
10 = Dark Red
11 = Violet
12 = Light Brown
13 = Medium Blue
14 = Dark Green
15 = Dark Pink
16 = Sky Blue
17 = Dark Brown
18 = Pink

**TIP: USE THE SUGGESTED COLOR PALETTE ON THE BACK COVER
FOR YOUR REFERENCE.**

# ARTWORK 8

0 = Black
1 = Dark Blue
2 = Medium Blue
3 = Dark Green
4 = Dark Orange
5 = Sky Blue
6 = Dark Grey
7 = Medium Green
8 = Dark Red
9 = Dark Brown
10 = Light Orange
11 = Tan
12 = Bright Green
13 = Light Blue
14 = Yellow Green
15 = Light Brown

**TIP: USE THE SUGGESTED COLOR PALETTE ON THE BACK COVER FOR YOUR REFERENCE.**

# ARTWORK 9

0 = Dark Green
1 = Light Blue
2 = Yellow Green
3 = Black
4 = Bright Green
5 = Medium Green
6 = Dark Brown

# ARTWORK 10

0 = Dark Brown

1 = Black

2 = Yellow Green

3 = Tan

4 = Light Brown

5 = Light Orange

6 = Sky Blue

7 = Medium Green

8 = Dark Orange

9 = Light Blue

10 = Yellow

11 = Bright Green

12 = Light Grey

13 = Dark Green

14 = Dark Grey

15 = Dark Purple

**TIP: USE THE SUGGESTED COLOR PALETTE ON THE BACK COVER FOR YOUR REFERENCE.**

# ARTWORK 11

0 = Tan
1 = Light Brown
2 = Light Blue
3 = Dark Green
4 = Bright Green
5 = Dark Brown
6 = Black
7 = Dark Red
8 = Cream
9 = Dark Orange
10 = Yellow Green
11 = Dark Grey
12 = Medium Green
13 = Sky Blue

# ARTWORK 12

0 = Cream
1 = Light Brown
2 = Black
3 = Pink
4 = Dark Brown
5 = Dark Pink
6 = Tan
7 = Red
8 = Dark Purple
9 = Yellow Green
10 = Sky Blue
11 = Violet
12 = Dark Blue
13 = Medium Blue
14 = Dark Red

TIP: USE THE SUGGESTED COLOR PALETTE ON THE BACK COVER
FOR YOUR REFERENCE.

- EMILY CLARKE COLORING BOOK -

# ARTWORK 13

0 = Black
1 = Dark Brown
2 = Tan
3 = Cream
4 = Light Blue
5 = Light Brown
6 = Yellow Green
7 = Dark Orange
8 = Dark Blue
9 = Violet
10 = Bright Green
11 = Medium Green
12 = Dark Red
13 = Dark Green

# ARTWORK 14

0 = Black

1 = Dark Orange

2 = Dark Grey

3 = Light Orange

4 = Light Grey

5 = White

6 = Dark Pink

7 = Dark Brown

8 = Pink

9 = Light Brown

10 = Cream

11 = Light Blue

# ARTWORK 15

0 = Black

1 = Bright Green

2 = Dark Green

3 = Yellow Green

4 = Medium Green

5 = Tan

6 = Dark Brown

7 = Cream

8 = White

9 = Light Blue

10 = Sky Blue

**TIP: USE THE SUGGESTED COLOR PALETTE ON THE BACK COVER FOR YOUR REFERENCE.**

# ARTWORK 16

0 = Black

1 = Dark Red

2 = Dark Green

3 = Dark Orange

4 = Medium Green

5 = Red

6 = Light Orange

7 = Dark Brown

8 = Yellow

9 = White

10 = Medium Blue

11 = Sky Blue

12 = Light Blue

# ARTWORK 17

0 = Dark Blue

1 = Black

2 = White

3 = Medium Blue

4 = Red

5 = Dark Red

6 = Sky Blue

7 = Dark Orange

8 = Light Grey

9 = Light Blue

10 = Light Brown

11 = Tan

# ARTWORK 18

0 = Black

1 = Dark Red

2 = Dark Orange

3 = Light Orange

4 = Dark Blue

5 = Yellow

6 = Sky Blue

7 = Dark Green

8 = Medium Green

9 = Cream

10 = Dark Purple

11 = Bright Green

12 = Yellow Green

13 = Dark Pink

14 = White

**TIP: USE THE SUGGESTED COLOR PALETTE ON THE BACK COVER FOR YOUR REFERENCE.**

# ARTWORK 19

0 = Sky Blue
1 = Yellow
2 = Light Orange
3 = Light Blue
4 = Dark Blue
5 = Pink
6 = Medium Blue
7 = Dark Orange
8 = Black
9 = Red
10 = Dark Pink
11 = Dark Red
12 = Dark Purple

TIP: USE THE SUGGESTED COLOR PALETTE ON THE BACK COVER
FOR YOUR REFERENCE.

- EMILY CLARKE COLORING BOOK -

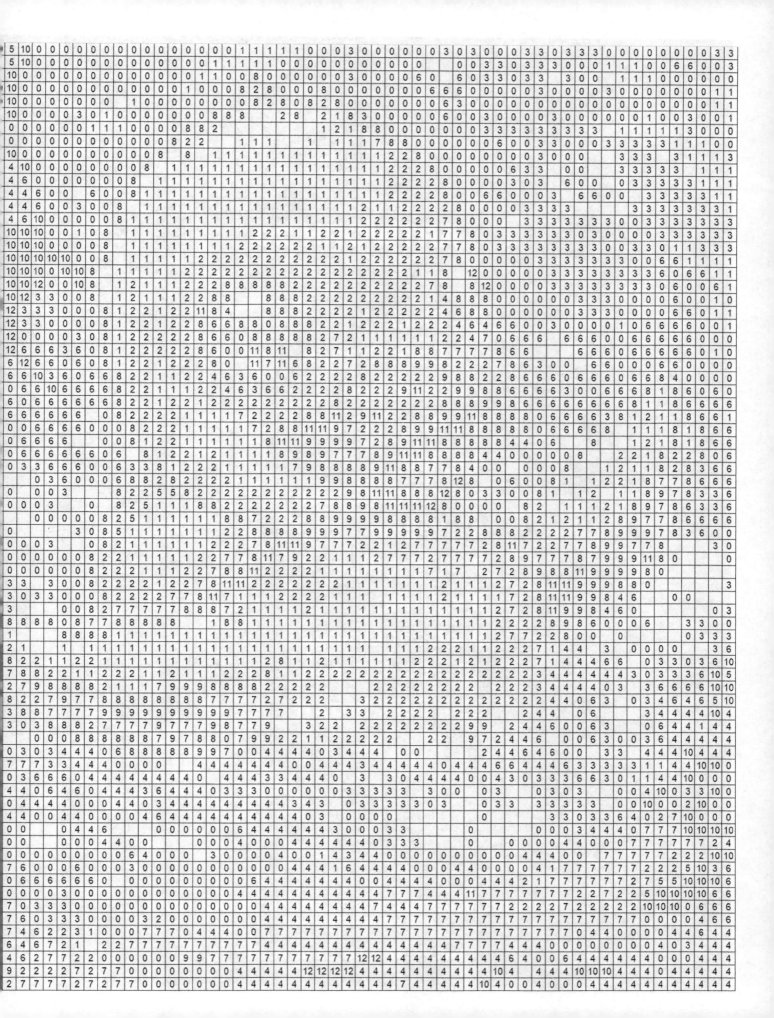

# ARTWORK 20

0 = Black

1 = Dark Orange

2 = Dark Red

3 = Bright Green

4 = Red

5 = Yellow Green

6 = Yellow

7 = Light Blue

8 = White

9 = Light Orange

10 = Dark Green

11 = Dark Brown

**TIP: USE THE SUGGESTED COLOR PALETTE ON THE BACK COVER
FOR YOUR REFERENCE.**

# ARTWORK 21

0 = Black

1 = Dark Red

2 = Red

3 = Light Orange

4 = Bright Green

5 = Dark Green

6 = Dark Orange

7 = Medium Blue

8 = Dark Blue

9 = Dark Brown

10 = Cream

11 = Yellow Green

12 = Light Brown

13 = Sky Blue

# ARTWORK 22

0 = Tan

1 = Sky Blue

2 = Light Orange

3 = Red

4 = Yellow

5 = Light Brown

6 = Cream

7 = Light Blue

8 = Dark Red

9 = Black

10 = Medium Blue

11 = Pink

12 = Dark Pink

13 = Bright Green

14 = Dark Purple

TIP: USE THE SUGGESTED COLOR PALETTE ON THE BACK COVER
FOR YOUR REFERENCE.

- EMILY CLARKE COLORING BOOK -

# ARTWORK 23

0 = Black
1 = Dark Grey
2 = Dark Green
3 = Dark Brown
4 = Medium Green
5 = Yellow Green
6 = Bright Green
7 = Dark Red
8 = Tan
9 = Dark Blue
10 = Light Brown
11 = Light Grey
12 = Yellow
13 = Light Orange
14 = Sky Blue
15 = Light Blue
16 = Violet
17 = Dark Orange

**TIP: USE THE SUGGESTED COLOR PALETTE ON THE BACK COVER
FOR YOUR REFERENCE.**

# ARTWORK 24

0 = Black
1 = Light Orange
2 = Dark Orange
3 = Dark Red
4 = Red
5 = Dark Brown
6 = Dark Blue
7 = Yellow
8 = Tan
9 = Light Brown
10 = Light Grey
11 = Dark Grey
12 = Violet
13 = Medium Blue
14 = Sky Blue

TIP: USE THE SUGGESTED COLOR PALETTE ON THE BACK COVER
FOR YOUR REFERENCE.

- EMILY CLARKE COLORING BOOK -

# ARTWORK 25

0 = Dark Blue
1 = Medium Blue
2 = Black
3 = Light Orange
4 = Sky Blue
5 = Medium Green
6 = Tan
7 = Light Grey
8 = Dark Orange
9 = Yellow Green
10 = Bright Green
11 = Dark Pink
12 = Yellow
13 = Light Blue
14 = Red
15 = Dark Purple
16 = Dark Green
17 = Light Brown
18 = Dark Red

# ARTWORK 26

0 = Bright Green
1 = Light Orange
2 = Dark Green
3 = Yellow Green
4 = Dark Brown
5 = Tan
6 = Dark Orange
7 = Medium Green
8 = Black
9 = Dark Red
10 = Light Brown
11 = Yellow
12 = Cream
13 = Sky Blue
14 = Dark Blue
15 = Dark Purple

# ARTWORK 27

0 = Black

1 = Light Blue

2 = Medium Blue

3 = Bright Green

4 = Light Grey

5 = Dark Grey

6 = Dark Green

7 = Sky Blue

8 = Medium Green

9 = Yellow Green

10 = Cream

11 = Dark Red

12 = Yellow

13 = Red

14 = Dark Purple

**TIP: USE THE SUGGESTED COLOR PALETTE ON THE BACK COVER
FOR YOUR REFERENCE.**

**- EMILY CLARKE COLORING BOOK -**

# ARTWORK 28

0 = Black
1 = Tan
2 = Dark Blue
3 = Dark Grey
4 = Yellow
5 = Light Grey
6 = Dark Pink
7 = Dark Purple
8 = Light Blue
9 = Dark Brown
10 = Dark Orange
11 = Violet
12 = Dark Red
13 = Cream
14 = Light Brown

# ARTWORK 29

0 = Black

1 = Dark Blue

2 = Dark Pink

3 = Red

4 = Dark Orange

5 = Cream

6 = Yellow

7 = Violet

8 = Dark Red

9 = Light Orange

10 = Medium Blue

11 = Dark Purple

12 = Pink

13 = Light Brown

14 = Medium Green

15 = Dark Brown

TIP: USE THE SUGGESTED COLOR PALETTE ON THE BACK COVER FOR YOUR REFERENCE.

# ARTWORK 30

0 = Black

1 = Dark Brown

2 = Dark Green

3 = Dark Orange

4 = Bright Green

5 = Tan

6 = Light Orange

7 = Yellow Green

8 = White

9 = Yellow

10 = Medium Green

11 = Light Blue

# ARTWORK 31

0 = Black

1 = Cream

2 = Dark Pink

3 = Dark Blue

4 = Dark Purple

5 = Dark Orange

6 = Light Orange

7 = Medium Blue

8 = Sky Blue

9 = Yellow Green

10 = Red

11 = Bright Green

12 = Pink

13 = Medium Green

14 = White

# ARTWORK 32

0 = Black
1 = Sky Blue
2 = Dark Brown
3 = Medium Blue
4 = Light Brown
5 = Tan
6 = Light Blue
7 = Dark Blue
8 = Dark Red

# ARTWORK 33

0 = Sky Blue
1 = Light Blue
2 = Medium Blue
3 = Dark Blue
4 = Black
5 = Pink
6 = Light Grey
7 = Violet
8 = Dark Purple
9 = Dark Grey
10 = Dark Pink

# ARTWORK 34

0 = Dark Blue

1 = Dark Pink

2 = Dark Orange

3 = Dark Purple

4 = Sky Blue

5 = Red

6 = Yellow Green

7 = Light Orange

8 = Yellow

9 = Medium Blue

10 = Black

11 = Light Blue

12 = Medium Green

13 = Bright Green

14 = Violet

15 = Dark Grey

16 = Light Brown

17 = Dark Brown

18 = Dark Green

**TIP: USE THE SUGGESTED COLOR PALETTE ON THE BACK COVER FOR YOUR REFERENCE.**

# ARTWORK 35

0 = Black

1 = Dark Blue

2 = Sky Blue

3 = Bright Green

4 = Dark Green

5 = Yellow Green

6 = White

7 = Light Blue

8 = Dark Orange

9 = Dark Red

10 = Medium Blue

11 = Light Orange

12 = Yellow

13 = Red

**TIP: USE THE SUGGESTED COLOR PALETTE ON THE BACK COVER FOR YOUR REFERENCE.**

Thank you for choosing this coloring book!
Please consider leaving a positive review on
Amazon. It would mean a lot to me and help
other customers find the book.
Your feedback is greatly appreciated!

★★★★★

🖤 Get Free Printable Coloring Pages 🖤
& Join Our Community!

https://linktr.ee/5ideas.publishing

- MAXIMUS PRIME -

THANK YOU!

TIP: USE THE SUGGESTED COLOR PALETTE ON THE BACK COVER
FOR YOUR REFERENCE.

- EMILY CLARKE COLORING BOOK -

# We are pleased to recommend
## our counterpart's wonderful coloring books

Made in the USA
Las Vegas, NV
01 December 2024

13141478R00044